DIRECTIONS IN DEV.

Water Markets
in the Americas

Larry Simpson
Klas Ringskog

The World Bank
Washington, D.C.

The findings, interpretations, and conclusions expressed in this study are
entirely those of the author and should not be attributed in any manner to the
World Bank, to its affiliated organizations, or to the members of its Board of
Executive Directors or the countries they represent.

Cover photograph: An irrigation project in Axochiapan, Mexico. Courtesy of
the Inter-American Development Bank

Library of Congress Cataloging-in-Publication Data

Simpson, Larry, 1937–
    Water markets in the Americas   /   Larry Simpson, Klas Ringskog.
        p.   cm.   —   (Directions in development)
    Includes bibliographical references.
    ISBN 0-8213-4088-3
    1. Water-supply—Economic aspects—America.   2. Water-supply—
Economic aspects—United States.   3. Water-supply—Economic
aspects—Canary Islands.   I. Ringskog, Klas, 1945–   .   II. Title.
III. Series: Directions in development (Washington, D.C.)
HD1693.S57   1997
333.91'009181'2—dc21   97-43069
                                                                                         CIP

Contents

Foreword

Water has become increasingly scarce worldwide, requiring careful economic and environmental management (World Bank 1993). In developing countries, the situation is exacerbated by rapid population growth and urbanization. As the demand for water for human and industrial use has escalated, so has the demand for water for irrigated agriculture. At the same time, the engineering and environmental costs are much higher for new water supplies than for sources already tapped. Moreover, governments have often misallocated and wasted water and permitted damage to the environment as a result of distorted policies, institutional weaknesses, market failure, and misguided investments. New challenges call for new approaches.

The Technical Department of the Latin America and the Caribbean Regional Office at the World Bank organized two regional seminars to explore the practical application of novel approaches for managing water resources. The first was held in Paris in June 1995 and was co-hosted by the French Agence pour la Cooperation Technique Industrielle et Economique. The second was held on the Canary Islands in June 1997 and was co-sponsored by the Municipality of La Laguna and by Aguas de Barcelona. In addition to the valuable insight gained from the presentations and discussions at these seminars, the World Bank and its borrowers are constantly learning from the experience gained through the water resources investment projects being implemented in countries such as Argentina, Brazil, Mexico, and Peru.

The seminars showed the great deal of interest that has developed throughout the economic and water resource management professions in the use of transferable water rights and markets to allocate scarce water efficiently. This interest has spawned widely varying claims as to the effectiveness of water markets and transferable water rights and their adaptability to the varying cultures and economic conditions of the developing world. It also has sparked a great deal of emotion from those who contrast such a commercial interpretation with the belief held by many cultures that water is a "gift from God" that should not be subject to allocation, private ownership, or dominion.

In order to bring a more balanced perspective to the debate, this volume summarizes the practice of using water markets to improve the efficiency of water use. The water sector is in a state of transition. Whereas in the past, water was regarded as public property, to be developed and operated by government agencies, the thinking is now shifting. It is now recognized that governments may make the greatest contribution not in building and operating public works but rather in creating the framework and the mechanisms that enable people and markets to use water more efficiently.

Foremost, users should be charged a price that reflects the true scarcity of water. Tradable water rights provide users with the incentive to use water wisely and steer it to its most productive use precisely because these rights endow water with a price or "opportunity cost." Users confident that their water property rights are secure are willing to make investments that increase the supply of water and convey it to where its returns are the highest.

Maritta Koch-Weser
Director
Environment, Rural, and
Socially Sustainable Development

Sri-Ram Aiyer
Director
Finance, Private Sector,
and Infrastructure

Acknowledgments

The authors would like to acknowledge the advice and contributions of the following individuals who provided peer review and assistance for this volume: John Briscoe (water resources economist, World Bank), Karin Kemper (water resources economist, World Bank), Luis Gabriel Azevedo (water resources engineer, World Bank), Emilio Custodio Gimena (director general, Instituto Tecnológico GeoMinera de España), and Paula Freitas (consultant, World Bank).

Larry Simpson is presently a consultant with the World Bank. He has extensive experience working in water resources management in the World Bank's member countries in Latin America as well as in China, India, and Morocco. He was previously the general manager of the Northern Colorado Water Conservancy District. Klas Ringskog is the principal water specialist in the Latin America and the Caribbean Regional Office of the World Bank.

Acronyms

CNA	Comisión Nacional de Agua (Mexico)
IID	Imperial Irrigation District (California)
MWD	Metropolitan Water District (Southern California)
PVID	Palo Verde Irrigation District (California)

1
Overview

As civilization approaches the next millennium, it is evident that one of the critical resources necessary for the health and well-being of the burgeoning world population is clean, reliable water for human consumption, food production, industrial production, and preservation of the ecological balance of nature. These competing uses create controversy but also opportunities for cooperation between governments, the private sector, and civil society. The sustainable management of water is imperative if society is to enter the next century with an improved standard of living and quality of life.

One of the keys to sustainable use of water is to educate leaders and the general population about the value and vulnerability of our limited water resources. In addition, a strong legal and institutional framework is needed to support the wise administration and management of water resources, and common sense, experience, and innovation are needed to develop and improve water resources management. These are the subjects of chapter 2. The ability of the market to allocate water to its highest and best use has been advocated by both economic theorists and practitioners in the field. The primary controversy between these two groups has not been whether markets should be used but, instead, the degree to which they should operate without regulation and governmental interference.

Chapter 3 presents the legal and institutional frameworks used to manage water resources in the Western Hemisphere. It compares the successes and pitfalls of these systems and spells out the foundations needed for sustainable management. None of these systems is perfect, but all provide lessons that can be used to refine the legal and institutional frameworks for managing water in other countries. Each cultural and geographical environment will have to adapt these principles carefully in order to achieve sound management of water resources.

Chapter 4 examines the legal and institutional frameworks and market concepts within the states of Colorado and California in the United States. These detailed comparisons show the difference in approaches between the mature, judicially regulated market system in Colorado and the more recent administratively regulated markets of California. In Colorado, water markets have evolved over the past 150 years with the heavy involvement of users and only limited involvement of government. The judicial system has been used to maintain fairness and equity within the market and to protect third-party beneficiaries. In this instance, the market process has evolved as an integral part of the development process.

In California, however, the market process has developed only recently in response to major water shortages precipitated by expanding demand, a lack of conservation practices, and a major drought. In this instance, the transfer of water rights in a market environment moved from being totally prohibited by law to being advocated by law. However, California adopted a highly regulated market with the government as the only qualified buyer and with prices set administratively. The first year of its use resulted in substantial financial losses for the state, which purchased large volumes of water at a set price only to have the demand for water evaporate as rains broke the drought. These purchases were concentrated in relatively limited areas, creating adverse social and economic consequences in the areas dried up as a result of this ad hoc market. The legislature and the responsible state agency subsequently modified both the law and the methodology in order to avert their undesirable consequences, but the process is still governmentally centered and highly regulated. At the same time, a form of bartering has developed among water resource institutions in the southern part of the state, and this provides valuable lessons for other areas.

Chapter 5, in a more abbreviated manner, examines the legal and institutional frameworks evolving in the Canary Islands and in Chile, Brazil, and Mexico in the Americas in order to compare some of the difficulties and successes encountered in these countries.

Although the Canary Islands do not lie within the Americas, their Spanish heritage is similar to that of Latin America. Moreover, market processes have evolved with strong private sector participation, and the management of this system involves, primarily, the use of groundwater in a unique island environment. The infrastructure, management methodologies, market processes, and institutional frameworks on these islands provide interesting concepts that may provide transferable lessons in the development and evolution of sustainable management practices.

Water markets in Chile have developed rapidly since 1973 as part of the deep reforms intended to make the water sector more efficient and to stimulate investments. The reforms culminated in the promulgation of the Water Code of 1981. Private parties can acquire water rights that are separate from land rights and are free to sell and buy water rights like any other property under the laws of the civil code. Efficiency gains have undoubtedly resulted from the growth of water trading. As could be expected, the development of water markets has not been without friction, and proposals have been made to amend the 1981 water code. The changes would oblige the holders of water rights to use them within five years or else forfeit them and would demand that greater attention be paid to the environmental costs related to the water released from hydroelectric and other dams.

Brazil has taken significant steps to develop sound legal and institutional frameworks for sustainable water resource management at both the federal and state levels. The recent adoption of a new federal water law and the adoption of similar laws in several states of the drought-stricken Northeast promise to modify both the allocation and management of water. These laws provide the foundations for the evolution of market-based allocation. In addition, a unique case within the State of Ceará in the Northeast is examined. This peer-regulated, market-oriented water management system has evolved over several centuries out of user necessity and without governmental regulation. This microcosm of cooperative management bears examination to evaluate some of the reasons for its success and to determine if some of the ideas are transferable.

In Mexico a highly centralized management and allocation system is becoming a more decentralized, user-oriented system. The basic foundations have been laid for sustainable management, and only time and evolution will determine the eventual success of the process. However, significant strides have been made, and valuable lessons can be derived by examining the methodologies employed.

Although using the market process to reallocate water to meet changing demands is an important tool of water management, it is, in fact, just one tool in the process. It does not supplant education, public information, a strong hydro-meteorological database, strong administration and enforcement of water use rights, or a strong legal and institutional framework. When supported by all of the above, a market process will assist in achieving the highest and best use for water resources.

2
Prerequisites for Successful Water Markets

Certain criteria or conditions must exist in order to transfer the use of water within a market framework. This chapter discusses these criteria as a prerequisite to developing both a functioning market in water use rights and the legal and administrative systems necessary to support it. The history and operation of water markets that have functioned with varying degrees of effectiveness for more than 100 years are presented in order to examine their successes and failures as well as the obstacles encountered as they moved from theory to reality.

Experience has shown that where apparent differences exist between supplies and demands and where the prerequisites exist for the market transfer of water use rights, water markets tend to evolve on their own. Much has been said about the market transfer of water use rights being the final answer to achieving efficiency in the allocation of rights. However, experience has shown that water markets are only one of many tools that must be in place and diligently pursued in order to achieve efficient use of water resources. The primary function of the market system is to allow supplies to meet changing demands in a manner that reflects the economic priority of competing demands. The following paragraphs discuss the prerequisites that enable water use markets to function either in a formal framework or on an informal basis.

There must be a definable product to trade in the market. This product must be capable of being controlled, measured, and traded as a commercial good. No market exists for sunshine, for example, because sunshine cannot be controlled and cannot be traded. A market in water use rights can only develop if ownership, quantity, measurability, and reliability are defined so as to generate confidence that the right is secure and viable.

Demand for water must exceed supply. In many regions, sufficient water exists so that there are no competing demands. However, demand changes over time, and supplies diminish as water quality deteriorates and seasonal imbalances in supply and demand create water scarcity. Shortages can arise naturally or be created artificially through control of the supplies. Even assuming that supply matches demand, the legislative or judicial processes can intervene to create shortages. For example, the California Supreme Court ordered the City of Los Angeles to give up 40 percent of its supply of water from the Owens River Valley (a source that had been used for more than 50 years) to repair alleged environmental damages. This decision caused an artificial imbalance—a shortage—in the water supply for Los Angeles even though demand did not increase. In a similar manner, an administrative decision at the federal level mandated that the U.S. Bureau of Reclamation reallocate 488 million cubic meters of water per year from the supply of the Central California Project to the Sacramento River to aid in the recovery of a species of small fish in the Sacramento delta. This created an immediate artificial shortage and increased the imbalance between supply and demand in that region. Such imbalances automatically increase the need for readjustment, and water markets provide an equitable way for water to move to its highest and best use in a fair and impartial process.

The supplies derived from use rights must be transported to where the water is needed and be available when needed. Water flowing in a river during times of flood or times of monsoon rain has little value for agricultural, municipal, or industrial use and, instead, generally represents a detriment to the overall system. However, the same water stored for use when rivers dry up becomes a valuable commodity. By the same token, water stored during wet years to stabilize supplies during drought years has a much greater economic value than water flowing freely in the river. From an environmental standpoint, however, the storage of water during wet years can cause ecological changes in the river, altering the riverine and riparian flora and fauna of the system. This ecological system has a value that is difficult to define in economic terms but that must compete with human and social uses of the water. Consequently, water at the right time and in the right place has an economic value, but creating this value may be accompanied by negatives. A market in water use rights can help to define these tradeoffs. A water resource capable of being stored, managed, and controlled can be optimized to meet the needs deemed most important by society. This water resource must have sufficient mobility to be transferred from the place of excess supply or storage to the place of economic use. This is accomplished through canals, pipelines, and, in some instances, mobile transportation. In fact, the less mobile a water use right is, the lower its value. The cost of creating such mobility by constructing infrastructure and developing other means of transportation must be included in the transaction costs that determine the economic value of the water use right in the marketplace.

As in any market system, there is an opportunity for abuse or imperfection in water markets. For a market to develop, *buyers must feel confident that they will receive and be able to use the right purchased.* The level of such confidence is reflected in the value of the right. For example, in capital stock markets, this confidence takes the form of an elaborate system of regulation, registration, and oversight. The stock exchanges are regarded as some of the most open markets in the world but still require a great deal of regulatory oversight. This is also the case with water use rights. For a market to exist in water use rights, there must be a system of allocation, permits, licenses, or property titling that is respected by the market. There must also be an administrative system that registers the ownership and title transfer of those rights and that polices and measures their use. Without a sufficiently strong system of regulation and administration through either a peer process or a governmental agency, buyers will not have sufficient confidence in their ability to receive the product for which they are paying.

The water rights system must also resolve conflicts, because disputes between the use and ownership of water use rights always seem to develop. Historically, conflict resolution has taken the form of peer group resolution, administrative arbitration, and recourse to the judicial system. This conflict resolution process must be viewed by the market as fair and impartial and must be capable of effective and timely action.

The system must also apportion supply during periods of shortages and excess. Although the market is the primary mechanism for apportioning supplies through both the permanent transfer and annual rental of use rights, the market must operate within a legal framework that defines the quantity of water available for use each year. The two legal frameworks discussed in this book are the riparian doctrine and the appropriation doctrine, specifically the prior appropriation system and the proportional appropriation system. A combination of these systems makes the initial allocations of historical use subject to equitable apportionment and issues subsequent rights on a prior appropriation basis. The alternative to these two methods is administrative apportionment by fiat, which has rarely proved equitable.

Most cultures and societies have assigned the use of water for human consumption precedence over all other uses. The other uses are then accorded varying degrees of preference within different types of legal systems. Although these preferences have social validity, a mechanism must be provided for compensating users whose rights are prescribed for higher preferences. Consequently, *well-defined and enforced mechanisms and criteria must be in place to assure that users are adequately compensated when their rights are confiscated or transferred to higher societal preferences.* Markets for water use rights can function efficiently for voluntary redistribution, particularly when a relatively free and efficient system of markets exists for the rental of surplus supplies. When shortages exist, opportunities for users with higher-preference uses to rent or purchase annual rights of use on the open market at the price determined by the market accommodate these preferences most equitably. The confiscation by fiat of agricultural rights for human supplies, for municipal and industrial supplies, or for flows to meet environmental demands has caused a great deal of unmitigated or uncompensated damage to the original users of the rights.

It is crucial in gauging the potential acceptability of water markets that the cultural and societal values of water resources be considered. Traditionally, throughout the world, many societies view water as a gift of nature or a gift of God, not subject to control, allocation, or dominion. In most countries, the legal ownership of a nation's water resources resides with the sovereign. This is the case in the United States and in most countries of the Americas. However, the sovereign may allocate or delegate the ownership, use, or control of that water to other subdivisions of government or to individuals, industries, and community groups. Water, because of its importance to mankind and its importance to the ecology of the earth, may take on an almost religious significance. This cultural and societal attitude must be considered when developing a system of water use rights and, more important, when developing a market in those rights. Education, public information, and user participation need to play a role in the development of this allocation process.

For any management program, including a market-based system, to succeed in the long term, it must be financially sustainable. The public education program must instill the concept that charges for use do not reflect a payment for a gift of nature. Instead, water charges should be countenanced as a payment to recover capital costs and provide sustainable funding for the administration, operation, and maintenance of the complex systems required to store, deliver, and administer the use of water in an equitable manner.

3
The Legal Foundations

Ever since water was first developed in the Middle East for use in the irrigation of crops and as potable water, the use of water has been subjected to some form of legal, administrative, or societal criteria. Legal matrices have evolved from religious sources, governmental processes, and peer limitations on the apportionment of use and the transferability of those uses. Water law systems in use today can be broken into two general categories: the riparian doctrine and the appropriation doctrine.

The Riparian Doctrine

The riparian type of legal system has been used primarily in regions where the supply of water exceeds the demand. This includes areas of high rainfall and river systems where flows are used primarily to support transportation, power generation, and waste assimilation as well as to supply water for human consumption and industrial purposes. Under this type of legal doctrine, a user has the right to extract water from the river system for use only on land adjacent to the river and only as long as the water is returned to the river undiminished in quantity or quality and in a manner that does not impair downstream use. This doctrine has many variants throughout the world but generally operates without any form of permit or regulatory administration. Disputes between users or uses are normally settled by the existing court or governmental dispute resolution processes.

In actual practice, few uses can meet this stringent criterion, because almost any use will diminish the quantity of water, if only through evaporation. In addition, almost all uses modify the quality or flow of the water supply. As long as the enforcement of this type of legal system rests principally on the potential injury to downstream users, the system has worked. However, in the eastern part of the United States where this type of water law predominates, the parameters have changed, and government has taken over responsibility for what was originally a function of the civil courts. Major pollution of river systems has necessitated governmental intervention, and the newly recognized concept of the river ecology itself as the downstream user has greatly modified the use of the pure riparian system. In actuality, the transbasin diversion of water from rivers, such as the transfer of water from the Delaware basin to the City of New York, could not have occurred under a pure riparian doctrine.

In most regions within the United States where riparian law is considered operative, it is replete with exceptions that allow water to be used on lands not adjacent to the river. Thus, even in the riparian system of the eastern United States, the allocation of use rights has been bartered, negotiated, or assigned by fiat to other users as demand both within and without river basins has exceeded supplies. In fact, a system where all riparian entities have the right to divert as much water as they reasonably need as long as it is returned to the river system relatively undiminished in either quality or quantity can only exist where supply far exceeds demand. The existence of water markets in a riparian system is improbable except in extremely localized instances or where the system is abandoned on an ad hoc basis to meet demands outside the basin.

The Appropriation Doctrine

The other legal doctrine commonly used to deal with the allocation and use of water is the appropriation doctrine. In this type of legal system, water use permits or licenses are issued to prospective water users to ensure their right to divert or store and use a certain quantity of water. The use of the water is not normally restricted to lands adjacent to the river, and water can be transported to another area or drainage for use away from the river. The exact structure of various appropriation systems differs throughout the world. The two systems in most common use are the prior appropriation type of system, which evolved over the past 150 years in some of the western states of the United States, and the proportional appropriation system, which involves licenses or permits for a proportional share of the available water within a basin or watershed. Both appropriation systems issue rights of use for varying periods of time. Some also issue perpetual usufructuary rights of use. Defined tenure permits or licenses are common in many Latin American countries, while perpetual property rights are more common in the western United States. The primary difference between these two appropriation systems is the manner in which they treat shortages of available water.

Prior Appropriation System

In the prior appropriation system, the first rights to be issued on the river have priority or seniority based on their date of origin. Rights that are issued later are the first to be curtailed during times of shortage. For example, in the prior appropriation system used in the State of Colorado in the United States, water use rights are issued as perpetual property rights. These rights are assigned priority based on their date of origin, with the earliest rights receiving the lowest number. In the event of shortages during the year or during a drought cycle, the right to divert water from the river is gradually curtailed beginning with the most junior or highest-number right and working down the priority numbers until there is sufficient water to satisfy the remaining active rights.

As long as the right is not changed substantially as to type of use, location of diversion, or quantity of diversion, it retains its priority and can be passed to other owners without restriction and without diminishing the value of its early date in the marketplace. If, however, a change in the use or diversion location creates injury to other rights, the right may be forced to subordinate its date or priority number to the junior rights that have been injured. A prior appropriation system would be very difficult to establish in a region that has few records of diversions or the timing of their origin because it would be difficult to establish the original dates of use. In a prior appropriation system, priorities have been established over time, as the region, such as Colorado, developed. To assign priorities arbitrarily and without a complete historic record would be extremely difficult, if not impossible.

Proportional Appropriation System

In a proportional appropriation system, permits or licenses are issued for the use of a fixed quantity of water, but the quantity of water available for the right is adjusted annually to reflect the availability of water within the basin or watershed. In this manner, all rights in a river basin share in any shortages or surpluses of water, regardless of when the rights were issued or developed. As each additional right is issued in a water-short system, the reliability and average yield of earlier rights become diluted. This can jeopardize the market value of rights because the yield of the right is unreliable.

An effective proportional system requires a well-organized administrative framework, a strong knowledge of the hydrology of the river basin, a well-developed hydro-meteorological information system, and

a well-organized participatory process to involve the users in management of the resource. Without a strong enforcement and measurement
system, users who are higher on the stream will inevitably take all the
water, leaving downstream users with little to show for their water use
right. Consequently, a proportional appropriation system requires a
strong institutional framework and a strong technology.

Combined System

Although the initial issuance of rights in a newly established legal system
with historical users is probably the best system unless clear priorities of
use can be historically determined, the use of a combined system that
issues all subsequent rights on a prior appropriation basis would protect
the original rights from dilution and allow the value of those initial rights
to remain reliable. This would prevent the damages that could be caused
by errors in estimating the overall safe yield of a basin and would allow
lower-value uses during wet years. High flows could also be stored
during wet years and used during droughts without damaging the initial
rights. This type of combined system would obviously complicate the
process of administering the rights but could be easily accommodated
through the use of computer technology.

Issuance of Water Use Rights

The manner in which rights are issued varies a great deal. For example,
water rights in Colorado are issued by a state water court to any person,
or entity, who demonstrates that he has put water to beneficial use in
accordance with the laws of the state. This is normally done in a two-step
process. A prospective water user can be issued a temporary or conditional water right that guarantees his place in line of priority for the
project or use intended. If and when the project is completed and the
water is put to beneficial use, the right is finalized by the water court
using the original appropriation date established under the conditional
right. This final right is then recorded by the state water administrator.
This type of system provides the prospective user with sufficient confidence to invest in building the infrastructure necessary to use the water
and in perfecting the right. The final water use right is then a perpetual
property right that endures beyond the original user and can be assigned
or transferred as long as the use and place of diversion do not change. A
contemplated change in use or place of diversion must be approved by
the water court after the public has been notified and all who feel they
might be injured by the change have an opportunity to present their

concerns to the court. This type of legal system, while eminently fair, can be complex and burdensome to administer.

In most other systems in the United States and in most Latin American countries, the issuance of water rights is an administrative process. In these types of systems, water use rights are issued by a government agency. The permits and licenses are generally issued for a fixed period of time, often with a conditional right of renewal and with no firm guarantee of future ownership of the right. In prior appropriation systems, the rights are placed in order of seniority based on when the right is issued. In the proportional system, each new right receives the same priority as the older rights and shares in the available water. If the administrator continues to issue rights beyond the safe yield of the basin, then the yield of each right is reduced proportionally. The administrative authority frequently limits the number of rights that can be issued in a basin based on safe yields determined from historical hydrological records or technical hydrology. This type of water rights issuance depends on the integrity and technical capability of the administrative authority. Frequently, this type of system uses the appellate courts as a last resort for resolving disputes.

An administrative system combined with a judicial appeals process can respond expeditiously to noncontroversial water use rights and, at the same time, provide the benefits of judicial arbitration of irreconcilable disputes. This type of water rights administration should function effectively in most developing-country situations.

Legal and Regulatory Framework

The legal systems governing the use and management of water resources and supporting a market in water use rights are complex and must be crafted to accommodate the cultural and social uniqueness of the society involved. In general, the laws should be kept as simple as possible, and the details should be spelled out in the regulations that implement the laws. The process of adopting or modifying the legal framework to support the market transfer of use rights should be recognized as evolutionary, and flexibility to adjust to unforeseen circumstances should be provided for, preferably in the regulations. The development of a solid legal framework supporting the allocation, administration, and enforcement of reliable water use rights is the first step in establishing the confidence necessary to support a market-based transfer system. Each of the examples regarding transferable water rights systems in the Americas involves, first and foremost, the adoption and implementation of a workable system of laws and regulations that will support both the use rights and the right to transfer those rights to other users and uses in a fair and equitable manner.

In most formal and informal legal systems, preference is based on the type of use. Water for human consumption always takes precedence over other uses in nearly all cultural settings. Beyond that, the preferences vary, with agriculture sometimes taking priority over industrial use and vice versa. For a preferential use system to maintain fairness, a user must be compensated when water is taken away from his particular use to satisfy a higher-priority use. In addition, care must be taken to assure, for example, that, in defining a legal preference for human use, water is not appropriated for general municipal purposes that include industrial, recreational, and landscaping uses.

Recent experiences in the development and implementation of legal and regulatory frameworks in countries such as Brazil, Chile, and Mexico provide lessons in the development of a model law. Although a water law must reflect the cultural, social, and climatological environment within which it will be implemented, a few basic concepts should be considered in any legal system for water.

There needs to be a definable right for the use of water under the water law. Whether this is in the form of a permit, license, or property right, the right should provide enough tenure to support and justify the investments made in constructing the necessary infrastructure and to assure the market that a right, if purchased, will continue to be viable.

There should be a requirement that the owner exercise efficient stewardship in using the right. In most legal systems, water rights have to be used for beneficial purposes. Many experts argue that this represents a subjective determination by an administrative authority or court and therefore a weakness in the system. However, experience has shown that without such a test of beneficial use or stewardship, monopolization of water is common. Others argue that a water market can take the place of such a beneficial-use test because inefficient users have an incentive under a market system to improve their efficiency and sell the excess rights. This has, in fact, occurred in the well-developed markets of the United States. However, the beneficial-use test has enhanced the management of water and in no way inhibited the development of strong market processes. The two concepts combine to enhance the efficient and sustainable management of water resources. In the final instance, the beneficial-use test adds checks and balances to prevent water from being appropriated purely to exercise political or economic power over river systems. Much has been said of the danger of including the beneficial-use test in a model water law. However, systems in which the beneficial-use test has been in place for long periods have provided the government and society with sufficient guarantees against flagrant misuse of water to allow market processes to develop without fear of monopolization.

The water law system must recognize all beneficial uses of water including human consumption, irrigation, industrial use, and the value of water for purposes such as environmental and aquatic preservation, hydroelectric generation, and navigation. The law must also be capable of considering and dealing with water quality, including methods of monitoring and controlling the discharge of pollutants into river systems and preventing the pollution of both surface and underground water supplies.

The inclusion of a mandatory water market within a proposed water law has frequently led to controversy and caused the law to be rejected in its entirety. A compromise providing for some form of transferability, even in limited form, can facilitate the eventual development of a water market. This is preferable to the all-or-nothing approach and provides time for the concept to become accepted. Ideally, this transferability mechanism should be market-based and as free of government interference as possible. However, from a practical viewpoint, allowing transferable rights with some form of administrative review is better than prohibiting them outright. Consequently, within a model water law, providing for transferability at a later date is preferable to having no water law at all.

A model water law should also set up an administrative enforcement system to provide for the sustainable administration of water use rights and to provide an administrative framework to support transferable rights. Ideally, this system should include processes for monitoring, measurement, administration, registration, and enforcement.

The water law should be kept basic and set out principles, with details to be spelled out and implemented through regulations. The regulatory system can be more easily modified and adjusted to meet changing needs than the formal water law. In the fervor to develop the water law, this regulatory process is frequently forgotten but is, in fact, even more important than the law itself. A model water law without good regulatory follow-through invites serious difficulties. It is through this regulatory process that the details of water allocation, water measurement, water transferability, and the freedom of the water market process can be developed.

The water law should provide authority for the collection of tariffs and use charges sufficient to assure the sustainable administration, operation, and maintenance of the system. Water charges can then be detailed in the regulatory process as long as the authority to collect them is provided for in the law itself.

The water law should clearly define any system of priorities or preferential uses. The regulations should then define the methods to be used in administering those preferences. In proportional appropriation systems, the law should also define the responsibility and authority for apportioning water during periods of shortage. The regulatory process can then deal with the details and technical requirements in a much more flexible manner than the law itself.

A water law should provide a mechanism within the legal system for making initial allocations for environmental purposes. It should also support a market in water use rights so that environmentally concerned entities can purchase rights on a willing buyer–willing seller basis in order to restore environmental values in highly developed river basins. It is also important to include the necessary enforcement and management mechanisms to assure that the rights to the water left in the river to preserve environmental values are respected on a par with all other water use rights.

The water law should clearly state the requirement for fair compensation in the event that use rights are appropriated for public purposes. Ideally, such appropriation should be discouraged, and the market process should be used to meet changing demands. Where possible, the confiscation of water use rights to meet political expediency should be made illegal. Even with such protection, the United States and Latin American countries are replete with examples of this having occurred.

One other key ingredient of a successful model law is the requirement that management of the resource be decentralized to the degree possible. Stakeholder involvement in the management and administration of water resources provides incentives for good management. Where the users are involved and where they depend on the water for their livelihood, they have historically exercised better stewardship than have administrative bureaucrats located outside the area. Consequently, a good water law requires the management and administration of water to be decentralized at least to the river basin level or lower, so that users and their representatives have the predominant say in how the resource is used. This type of stakeholder involvement can be provided for and mandated by law. The regulatory process should be used to detail this participatory process.

The question of whether the water law should be at the federal, state, or provincial level should also be addressed. In some countries, such as the United States, the constitution and the federal law spell out this relationship. The federal law should define the rights of the lower levels of government to legislate and regulate the use of water. In most countries, including the United States, the ownership of water rests with the sovereign. However, the right to allocate and manage water can be delegated by the sovereign to the lower levels of government, as it is in the United States. The state or provincial water laws can then spell out the basic principles under which the resource will be allocated, used, and managed in accordance with the specific conditions and needs of users in the state.

4
Water Markets in the United States

Water markets in the United States have developed mainly in the dry, southwestern states. Rapid economic growth was forced to confront the scarcity of water early on, which stimulated the trading of water rights. Water markets have reached their fullest development in Colorado, whose tradition of trading water rights goes back 150 years. More recently, California has also promoted exchanges of water rights, albeit with greater direct government control. The lessons learned as trading has developed are valuable for many developing countries, where economic growth is confronting many of the same issues related to water.

Colorado

Colorado law places water rights within the prior appropriation doctrine under the jurisdiction of the courts through a special water court established in each judicial district of the state. This water court reviews evidence with regard to an application for a water use right and considers the objections voiced by parties that feel they could be injured by the exercise of that right. The court then makes the decision regarding the application on both a conditional basis and, after diversion and beneficial use, on the final decree for a perfected water right. To aid the judiciary in this function, the state has an administrative process for measuring, monitoring, and enforcing water rights. The administrative function is performed by local river commissioners under the jurisdiction of a state engineer who monitors and measures water use and enforces the water laws of the state. This official also keeps a complete record of hydrologic and water rights.

While the state retains ownership of the water resource, that water is allocated to users who can put the water to beneficial use. Once a conditional water right has been issued, the recipient has a period of time in which to develop and put that water to beneficial use. During that period he is required to, periodically, report to the court and show diligence in the effort to develop and use the right. If the owner of a conditional right fails to prove diligence, the conditional right may be dismissed. When the owner of either a conditional or a final water use right wishes to transfer that right to another owner, he may do so, as with any other property right. Court or state approval is not required for such a transfer. However, if a change of use or change in point of diversion is contemplated, the entity seeking to modify the right must file an application with the court. This application is then published in broadly distributed newspapers of the area so that all who feel that they might be injured have an opportunity to present their concerns before the court. If the alleged injury is proven, then the court must determine adequate remedies or compensation to prevent third-party damages. If there are no protests and the change in use or change in diversion is deemed to be reasonable, the court typically grants the change. Such official changes commonly represent major modifications of the original intended or historic use of the water right. These changes include transbasin diversions, diversions from agricultural use to municipal use, or other modifications that could have a strong third-party impact. Although cumbersome, this process is eminently fair, giving all persons who feel they might be injured an opportunity to present their concerns before an impartial court.

Based on historical experience, this process has worked well in Colorado. However, because water law is evolving based on case law and legal precedents, the law has changed over time to accommodate changes in use that are recognized by society. An example of this are the minimum stream flow rights within rivers protected and preserved by the State Water Conservation Board. Another recent example, in the instance of new inbasin rights and transbasin diversion or "new basin water," applicants have applied for rights to use water for all purposes and for jurisdiction over all return flows. Even if the return flows are used, the right to those return flows cannot be prescribed. This bestows the right to trade water freely without compensable injury to third-party users. This is the case with the contractual shares of the Colorado/Big Thompson Transbasin Diversion Project. The right to the return flows was given to downstream users with the stipulation that no rights could accrue to the users of the return flows. This has, historically, allowed an extremely free market without concern for third-party impacts. This has

increased the market valuation of the shares many times and has provided an easily transferred water supply to meet changing demands
without having to resort to court actions.

Colorado water law has evolved to include the conjunctive use of
groundwater and surface water in areas where the two are integrally
connected. In addition, in nontributary groundwater basins where there
is no significant connection between surface water and groundwater
resources, the law has been modified to provide for the management and
allocation of rights to ensure that each user has a proportional share of
the resource. In essence, this is a proportional appropriation system.
These rights are generally associated with the overlying land, and all
users share equally in the extraction of the groundwater. Groundwater
law in Colorado developed somewhat later than surface water law.
Groundwater law was required because large irrigation wells were
being placed in alluvial aquifers immediately adjacent to rivers. Extrac-
tions from these wells depleted the surface flows of water during
droughts as unregulated irrigation wells were pumped without limitations. As a consequence, the water law was modified to require that all
wells in aquifers connected to surface supplies be adjudicated and
administered in the priority system along with surface water rights.

Because most surface water rights were developed between 1876 and
1920, and most wells were drilled after 1950, nearly all wells in conjunctive aquifers were junior to the surface water rights. As a consequence,
their use was the first to be curtailed during periods of shortage. To
circumvent this problem and use the valuable underground storage
during droughts, augmentation plans were developed whereby well
owners associations could purchase or rent the rights to surface water.
This process uses the water market to its fullest. In addition, the well
owners associations provide users of surface water with underground
water pumped from the aquifer during periods of drought. These augmentation plans are fairly innovative, because permanent purchases,
annual rental of rights, and a system of recharge credits for artificial
recharge are used to offset infringement on senior surface rights. This
integrated system contributes to the conservation and management of
water resources and, at the same time, allows optimal use of vast
underground water systems to stabilize regional water supplies during
droughts.

The Colorado/Big Thompson Scheme

The history of water right transactions in Colorado largely reflects the
growth of the municipal industrial complex along the state's front range.

Since 1961 the price for a contractual right to use one unit of water from the Colorado/Big Thompson water scheme in the northeastern front range has escalated (see figure 4.1). After the project was completed in the 1950s, the annual assessment was at a marginal point, because many farmers thought that the water provided by a contractual right-of-use unit or that a share of the Colorado/Big Thompson scheme was not worth its price. Moreover, some worried that the lien placed on their farms to guarantee repayment of the capital cost of the project might be foreclosed if the district did not pay its obligations. During this period, transfers and sales were conducted at extremely low values. However, in the early 1960s, rural water districts were formed to provide potable water to rural communities and farmers in Northern Colorado. These districts also provided water for the region's growing cattle feedlot industry. As each district was formed, it chose to rely totally on the easily accessible Colorado/Big Thompson units. These units were the obvious choice because they were available without the threat of third-party damages and were capable of delivering stored water on demand. In addition, they could be purchased a few at a time, as demand increased, thus avoiding the need to pay the large capital costs of developing new supplies before the bulk of water was needed. As these water rights were purchased, the value of the units rose rapidly.

Figure 4.1   Price per Unit of Water from Colorado/Big Thompson Scheme, 1961–97

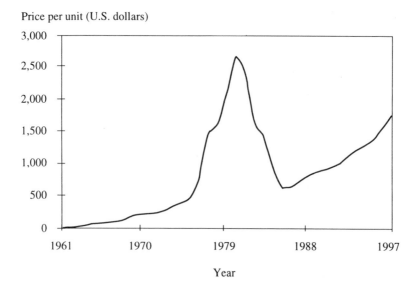

Price per unit (U.S. dollars)

Year

In many instances, professional water brokers moved into the market and purchased farms from unsuspecting farmers who did not understand the value of their water supplies. These brokers then sold the units of Colorado/Big Thompson water for sufficient profit to pay for purchase of the farms. For a period of three or four years, farmers sold off their capital assets without realizing their value in the marketplace. Once transparency developed through word of mouth and published information, farmers became reluctant to sell their water, which they began to view as one of their strongest assets.

At that same time, many lien holders, bankers, and mortgage companies began to attach liens on the water as well as the land in an effort to retain the water on the land as security against the mortgages. In the event of default, lenders could quickly sell the water to recover the value of the loans. Through this process, banks began to recognize the high value of water related to land. Without irrigation water, the lands in this dry region were worth very little, unless they were located in the path of development.

Once the initial impact of the rural domestic water districts had been absorbed by the market, the value of units of Colorado/Big Thompson water flattened out until 1970. During the next 15 years, several large industrial buyers entered the market as large electronic industries moved into the region. This created a strong demand for water as the growing municipalities began to compete for water supplies through the Colorado/Big Thompson units. During this period, the unit price escalated to approximately $2,800 in 1980 ($3.28 per cubic meter).

The value of this source of supply eventually reached a point where six of the larger municipalities began searching for a more economical source of water. In addition to the rising cost of the units, these cities recognized that the valuable agricultural economy was drying up and that this was having a negative impact on their own economies.

The Windy Gap Project

In 1969 these cities decided to bring supplemental water from the Colorado River basin to the existing storage and diversion facilities of the Colorado/Big Thompson project. Using the existing transmission capacity of the Adams Tunnel component of the Colorado/Big Thompson scheme, the Windy Gap Project was able to capitalize on this 21-kilometer-long, 3-meter-diameter tunnel through the continental divide to bring water to the eastern slope for municipal and industrial purposes. With the value of a unit of Colorado/Big Thompson water with an average yield of 854 cubic meters costing $3.28 per cubic meter, a unit of the Windy Gap water, at $2.05 per cubic meter, was deemed to be the most economical choice. As a consequence, this project was constructed and completed in 1985.

During this period, many speculators entered the market, buying the fast-escalating Colorado/Big Thompson units for investors, some of whom even placed these assets in their retirement accounts. However, as should have been anticipated, when the Windy Gap Project was completed, municipalities that had been driving the market demand suddenly left the market as they received assurance that Windy Gap would meet their future demand for water. At the same time, escalating interest rates caused many farmers to sell water to pay mortgages and debt. The price of a unit of Colorado/Big Thompson water plummeted, reaching approximately $1.05 per cubic meter at one point in 1990. Those who had invested in this asset expecting limitless capital growth suffered substantial losses.

This region continued to grow, and the Windy Gap supply was absorbed into the system or sold by some of the municipalities, which then bought more undervalued Colorado/Big Thompson units. Windy Gap water was sold to municipalities within the Denver metropolitan area that did not have access to the Colorado/Big Thompson water. This allowed the Windy Gap participants to capitalize on the price differential. The previous provincial concerns with preserving water supplies for the Northern Colorado area evaporated in the face of the large price differentials and the opportunity to make a profit. Over this period of time, immigration into the area from other parts of the United States changed public opinion, and provincial loyalty to the area largely disappeared.

With this increase in competition, the value of a unit of Colorado/Big Thompson water escalated once again. Equilibrium in the market is expected when a unit of Windy Gap water is equivalent in value to the same quantity of Colorado/Big Thompson water. Because the two supplies are not equivalent in reliability, the market will sort out the value of this difference based on the buyer's and seller's perception of it. This market history and the reasons behind the variation and escalation of prices in the market offer an excellent example of the manner in which a water market can effectively operate and enable supplies to adjust to changing demands.

The City of Thornton Scheme

During this same period, Thornton, a suburb of Denver, pursued another alternative, entering the market for shares of stock in the privately held water supply and storage company, located in the Cache La Poudre River basin. This city had purchased, through a dummy corporation, approximately 47 percent of the outstanding shares of the stock and farms under this irrigation company before being discovered as the buyer. At this point, the company's remaining stockholders refused to sell further shares to the city, leaving the city in a minority position. The city filed extensive litigation seeking to divert water from the river basin to the city and to change use of the water to municipal use. Protesters in this litigation included the Northern Colorado Water Conservancy District, which provides an augmentation supply to the region, many downstream users and user districts, return-flow users in the immediate area, and the remaining shareholders of the ditch system.

One of the principal concerns of the other shareholders was that the ditch would no longer have sufficient water to compensate for seepage and evaporation. This litigation lasted for many years and resulted in the city eventually receiving the right to transfer about 50 percent of the historic water supply that it had purchased. The remainder was required to be left either in the ditch to alleviate seepage and evaporation or in the river to satisfy downstream return-flow rights. In essence, the city was restricted to the consumptive use of water. Thornton was also required to guarantee that extensive mitigation would be conducted to rehabilitate the dried lands to prevent wind erosion and the growth of noxious weeds. The city still must construct an extremely expensive, long pipeline and pumping system 90 kilometers south to its boundaries. In hindsight, perhaps the city should have purchased shares of the Windy Gap Project as their neighboring suburban cities did or should have negotiated an agreement with irrigation companies closer to its boundaries that were already being absorbed by the city's expanding municipal development. In the end, the cost of the stock transactions, the infrastructure, and the mitigation will probably far exceed the cost of either Windy Gap or any alternative supplies of water.

This is an excellent example of how transaction costs resulting from third-party impacts affect the market value of water supplies in the market. The market quickly sorts out these costs and values the alternative supplies based on the real costs of making the purchased supplies usable. Water that is in storage and can be delivered on demand in a reliable manner has a high value in the market, while "opportunity water" that is available only during high runoff periods and must be transported long distances has low value. The experienced buyer who operates from a position of knowledge and information quickly understands this differential value and adjusts the offering price to reflect it.

This also indicates that the market system seldom provides a cheap bargain. In the water markets of Colorado, the principle of caveat emptor or "buyer beware" is alive and well. Advocates of free market transfer of water use rights frequently look at this type of transaction cost as an impediment to the free market. However, rather than being an imperfection, it is actually the market in action and is the primary reason that a market system provides the best and fairest mechanism for transferring water use. It is the only mechanism that automatically takes into account the real value of peripheral and indirect costs as long as full knowledge and transparency are available.

At the local or individual level and in the short term, the market mechanism may not reflect the true impacts to a region when a transbasin diversion of supplies begins to affect the economic spin-off or multiplier benefits to regions in the basin of origin, the secondary users of the water, or the environment. In the short term, a free market does not assure that mitigation of all these damages will be compensated and may not reflect the true cost of the loss of water supply to an area. Although cumbersome, using the courts to resolve conflicts and assure compensation for damages incurred in a market transaction does allow most affected entities to have their day in the court. Historically, the water courts have exercised careful and objective judgment in the analysis of damages and, at the same time, have allowed great flexibility in adjusting to the changing demands generated through the market process.

Interstate Transfers

Water use in Colorado is also subject to interstate restrictions. Colorado is the headwaters state for many interstate river systems, including the Colorado River, the Rio Grande River, the Arkansas River, the South Platte River, and the North Platte River, all of which flow into other states. The use of water in the state has historically been subjected to apportionment of the river flows to the downstream states. This process was initially started through a court adjudication in federal court in 1902 between the states of Colorado and Kansas with regard to the Arkansas River, followed in 1922 by an adjudication among the states of Wyoming, Nebraska, and Colorado with regard to the North Platte River. This latter adjudication apportioned the greater part of the flows of that river system to Wyoming and Nebraska, with Colorado receiving only a minimal share of the water supply.

These "equitable apportionment" actions by the federal court caused a great deal of concern among all of the states in the various river basins. Rather than allow the courts to make such decisions, the states immediately began negotiating compacts for the apportionment of basin yields. Consequently, compacts were negotiated on the South Platte River, the Rio Grande River, and the Colorado River. These interstate compacts were then submitted to the federal courts for ratification. Over the years, these compacts have been subjected to frequent court interpretations and litigations between states, the most recent being litigation between Kansas and Colorado with regard to the amount of water that residents of Colorado take from the Arkansas River. Similar litigation has occurred between Arizona and California, with Arizona winning a limitation on Southern California's historic use of water from the Colorado River.

These compacts are significant with regard to water markets in that legal authorities proclaimed that the sale of water rights between states either by individuals or by the states would void the provisions of the compacts. If the compacts were no longer valid, the entire river system could be subjected to an open market process. On the Colorado River, one of the major purposes of the compact was to allow the slower-developing states, such as Colorado, Utah, and Wyoming, time to develop and to place their proportional shares of the basin water to beneficial use, while being protected from the voracious appetites of the faster-developing downstream states of Arizona, California, and Nevada. A market system allowing water to be sold to the lower basins would adversely affect the economic future of the upstream states in exchange for short-term gains. Although in economic theory this might be the highest and best use of the water in the short term, it would cause the upper-basin states to lose one of their most valuable resources for future development. This issue is being hotly debated and will continue to be subjected to political and economic pressure. As the need for water continues to expand in Southern California, the Las Vegas (Nevada) area, and the metropolitan complexes of central Arizona, the upper-basin states will continue to be pressured to allow their users to sell water rights to the lower basin.

The Lessons Learned

A few conclusions can be drawn from Colorado's experience with water markets:

- The existence of water use rights as personal property rights that are transferable in the open market has resulted in a successful marketplace that allows water to seek its highest value and, at the same time, allows the system to adjust to changing priorities and demands.

- This water market system has not resulted in large water monopolies. As with any other market, the risks involved in speculation and the accumulation of large blocks of water at prices set by the market have been balanced by the drop in market values as newly developed water supplies have been added to the system.
- The water market and the water laws that support it must remain dynamic and capable of evolving to meet changing situations and changing needs. Rigidity in the market caused by tradition or the inability of the legal system to adjust reduces the market's effectiveness and, in the long run, causes less-than-optimal use of scarce water supplies.
- Experience has shown that water rights should meet a beneficial-use test. The recognized beneficial use may be adjusted over time to meet changing societal priorities such as recognition of environmental concerns as a beneficial use, but the wise use of such a test prevents abuse and misuse of this precious resource.
- Water use rights for environmental purposes, including instream flows, recreation, and aesthetic values, should be considered a beneficial use and be recognized in the allocation of initial water rights. Legal provision should be made to allow the marketplace to be used to restore water to the rivers for these purposes.
- In market transfers where third-party beneficiaries may be injured, a fair and impartial system must be established that allows the buyers and sellers of water rights to pursue their transactions but that also allows the parties affected by those transactions to have their concerns considered and mitigated or compensated where valid. The process should be such that, in the end, the market reflects all the costs of the transfer, including the cost of all damages to others.
- The value of water within a market system depends on the primary factors of reliability, availability on demand, mobility, and indirect transaction costs. There must be a strong administrative system that monitors, measures, registers, and enforces the water rights so that both the buyer and the seller can be assured that their investment will be honored. With such assurances, an active and reliable market can exist.
- Historically, transactions in water rights only result if demand exceeds supply in certain areas. In Colorado, this initially meant the exchange of water among irrigation companies. However, as large metropolitan areas expanded and a strong environmental movement inhibited the development of new water resource systems, the demand for water grew enough to offset the high transaction costs

of basin-of-origin compensation, mitigation of injury to third parties, and high legal and technical costs.

- Transparency and a high degree of education and public information with regard to the market processes and the value of a water use right should exist in order for a market to function properly. These evolve slowly over time, and a great deal of caution and care must be taken to implement public education and to inform all the owners of water use rights of the value of those rights.

- A water market system can be facilitated through the use of mediators and brokers who bring the buyers and sellers together. While private entrepreneurs frequently function as brokers for permanent transfers, the water users organization responsible for maintaining records and operating a system can provide a central clearinghouse for renting water use rights on an annual basis.

- Because of the complexities sometimes involved in water use transfers, the process cannot be simplified greatly without jeopardizing the rights of others. Although caution should be taken, efforts should be made to minimize bureaucratic discretion and the need for legal advice and to ensure that undisputed transfers can happen simply and quickly.

- Lastly, the ownership and use of water are often emotional issues that involve the political process, particularly in a dry area. Consequently, a market transfer process free of political interference will require the education of persons in positions of political power and leadership within the communities and the government as well as the general population. The use of water resources is also a highly visible subject that politicians and advocates will frequently use to accomplish other objectives. The only way to prevent such misuse of power is to ensure that the public is informed.

In summary, the Colorado water market system, which has functioned effectively for more than 150 years in a variety of formats, provides a learning experience that is transferable to other regions and cultures. The concepts at work in Colorado remain basically the same even though the localities and cultures change. However, they must be adapted to the cultural and social environments involved.

California

The State of California uses three types of water law. The northern part of the state is relatively humid and has historically used the riparian doctrine. In contrast, the deserts of Central and Southern California use the prior appropriation doctrine, which basically descended from California mining laws. The prior appropriation system was necessary to divert water from river systems to the most fertile lands and mining claims where water was needed. The third type of water law descended from a Spanish water law called the Pueblo Doctrine. Under this form of law, a city that can trace its origin as a Spanish pueblo to the period in which California formed part of the Spanish territories can avail itself of the pueblo entitlement. This entitlement allows the pueblo or its descendant city the right to all of the water in perpetuity that is generated from the river basin in which it is situated. The City of Los Angeles, an original Spanish pueblo, has such an entitlement to the Los Angeles River. Even though upstream cities may have used water from the Los Angeles River historically, Los Angeles expropriated all of the yield of the river as its needs grew. The Pueblo Doctrine is an anomaly and is sufficiently unique as to have little significance for water management and water markets today. However, water law and water markets must be clearly divided between the relatively humid northern portion of the state and the very dry areas of Southern California.

This multifaceted legal system has created frequent conflict. For example, when the California Water Resources Project was proposed to divert water from the riparian areas of Northern California to the central basin and Southern California, the riparian doctrine that existed in the northern areas had to be modified to allow this massive transbasin diversion. However, this same riparian doctrine carries with it the concept of a public trust residing in the state and requiring water supplies to be used for the benefit of the general public. In recent years, California state courts were faced with strong political and environmental pressure demanding that Los Angeles curtail its diversion of water from the Owens Valley located in the southern desert region. These advocates were attempting to restore the environmental integrity of the highly saline Mono Lake. The California State Supreme Court invoked the riparian-derived public trust doctrine to mandate that Los Angeles forgo these diversions to allow the lake to be restored to its natural state.

To add to the complexity of the water law within California, the state is riparian to the Colorado River and receives a share of the water apportioned under the 1922 Colorado River Compact. The state immediately diverts the water from that basin for use in the Imperial Valley and coastal basins according to the mobility concept of the appropriation doctrine. Being the state farthest down the river and with the fastest growth rate, California has been using not only its share of the Colorado River water but, through default, much of the apportioned share of the slower-growing upstream states. The Colorado River Compact was set up to protect the apportioned shares of those states as the demands of California, Arizona, and Nevada grew rapidly.

The Southern California Metropolitan Water District constructed a massive system for transporting bulk water from the Colorado River to Southern California coastal basins located on the other side of the Pacific coastal range. In effect, the Colorado River became a lifeline for growth in Southern California. During the 1960s, major litigation between Arizona and California occurred over the apportionment of the lower-basin share of the compact water. As a result of this litigation, California's share of the lower-basin apportionment was limited a great deal from its historic use. The apportionment of Arizona was set at a level sufficient to develop the massive Central Arizona Project intended to provide water for the cities of Phoenix and Tucson and for agricultural purposes. Although this solution was the result of a court decision and legislative action at the federal level, politics played a large part in the decision, as upper-basin states joined Arizona in fashioning a compromise in exchange for federal commitments to develop additional federal projects in the upper basin.

As a consequence of this reapportionment, the southern part of California decided to pursue the California Water Project, which would bring water from tributaries of the Sacramento River in the north through a large system of canals and pumping plants to the central basin and Southern California. The water rights for this massive project were issued through legislative and administrative action. The project was constructed in the 1960s and 1970s and is relatively complete at this time. However, the peripheral canal system around the Sacramento delta was never constructed. At present, water is stored in Oroville dam on the north end of the system, released into the Sacramento River, and then diverted once again into the aqueduct system that carries it to Central and Southern California. This massive transbasin diversion merged the concepts of the appropriation and the riparian doctrines and could not have been accommodated within the riparian doctrine without special exception.

Market Transfers

With regard to the development of major water markets within California, state law generally has historically precluded such market transfers. The owner of a water right did not originally have the freedom of transfer because, until recently, the law was interpreted to mean that a water user who attempted to sell or transfer a right had demonstrated that he no longer had a beneficial use for the water and, consequently, had technically abandoned the right and was forced to relinquish it. In 1914 the State Water Resources Control Board was formed with the authority to issue permits for the use of water supplies. Historically, the state board held that water rights could be transferred but that the state board would decide whether a transfer right could affect all other uses. Because the state water board was responsible for maintaining return flows, its actions tended to discourage transfers.

This situation continued until specific legislation in 1980 clarified that sale of a right did not indicate abandonment or nonbeneficial use of the water. Throughout the 1980s, the state legislature continued to pass additional bills in an attempt to create a water market. This included establishment of a program to facilitate long-term water transfers by setting up a data bank of entities interested in conducting water transfers. The new law also replaced the state board with the Department of Water Resources and required that this agency and all other public water agencies make available a portion of unused capacities in water conveyance facilities to facilitate the mobility of water transfers. In 1991, in response to a major drought, the state legislature passed emergency legislation creating a drought water bank within the Department of Water Resources. This water bank provided for the buyback of water supplies from the holders of water use rights as a temporary measure to offset the effect of the drought.

The idea was to develop a permanent program for buying water use rights and renting them on an annual basis to maintain a controlled water bank. This idea was not totally new. During the 1976 and 1977 drought, the U.S. Bureau of Reclamation established a water bank in the Central Valley Project that bought more than 57 million cubic meters of water within the system at an average value of $40.00 per thousand cubic meters. It then sold this water to other users within the project who had critical needs, for an average value of $41.00 per thousand cubic meters. This water bank primarily provided emergency water supplies to maintain the viability of orchards or perennial crops that might have been lost otherwise, with devastating economic effects.

The state water bank was established primarily to meet the emergency conditions of the 1987 to 1992 drought. The Department of Water Resources purchased more than 975 million cubic meters of water at an average price of $102.50 per thousand cubic meters. Administrative rules established prices based on estimates of what the selling farmers could have received if they had used that water to grow high-value crops, plus an incentive to facilitate the trade. The Department of Water Resources expended approximately $100 million for this water bank. The water assembled in the bank was then sold for a value of $144.00 per thousand cubic meters plus the cost of transportation, primarily to high-value agricultural purposes and to critical urban needs. Of the water sold from the bank, 80 percent went to municipal users in Southern California and in the San Francisco Bay area.

However, the Department of Water Resources sold less than half of the water purchased, because hydrologic conditions changed, and rains began in March of that year. The excess water was, instead, used to mitigate water quality problems in the Sacramento delta. The State Water Project also came to the rescue with a purchase of 325 million cubic meters for approximately $40 million. It stored the water for eventual delivery to contractors in the state project system.

Although the overall economic value of this highly regulated and controlled water market was deemed to be positive and beneficial, the results of the process are still under debate. There were adverse impacts on indirect beneficiaries of water supplies in certain regions, and the program caused losses to the general economies of some areas due to the fallowing of more than 69,000 hectares of agricultural land. The cost of unemployment and social services in those regions escalated. The jurisdictions involved made claims against the Department of Water Resources for the costs sustained, but compensation has yet to be provided. In addition, environmentalists charged that the drastic modification of cropping patterns caused the loss of food and habitat for water fowls, because crops were no longer available for this purpose. In addition, modifications of return-flow patterns depleted instream flows, with adverse impacts on wildlife within these areas.

Operation of the water bank in the following year was reduced in scale because of the increased precipitation, with the purchase of only 232 million cubic meters of water at $61.00 per thousand cubic meters derived primarily from groundwater exchanges. Fallowing of land was not involved, and, in this instance, the Department of Water Resources purchased the water only after finding a willing buyer who would commit in writing to purchase those supplies. The concept of a water bank is still officially in place, and the Department of Water Resources continues to investigate the use of water banks to mitigate the adverse consequences of drought. The idea of a highly regulated market will undoubtedly continue to be used to stabilize water supplies and may well result in a more rational process in subsequent years. However, any advantage of such a regulated system over a free market is difficult to observe, and the disadvantages are obvious.

Another interesting concept of water transfer in relation to the market process has been evolving over the past few years through negotiations between the Southern California Metropolitan Water District (MWD) and the Imperial Irrigation District (IID), both major users of Colorado River water and located in the extreme south desert region of the state. IID has historically diverted a large quantity of water from the Colorado River as part of California's apportioned share under the Colorado River Interstate Compact and has used that water to irrigate high-value food crops. Irrigation in the IID has been relatively inefficient, and the economic incentive for using more efficient techniques has not existed until now. However, with the demand for water increasing, an agreement was reached following lengthy negotiations whereby MWD would pay up to $200 million for conservation measures to improve the distribution system and irrigation technologies within the IID. In payment for these improvements, MWD would receive 122 million cubic meters of the conserved water per year for a period of 35 years. The water lost due to inefficient irrigation ends up in a saline basin called the Salton Sea. As a consequence, the use of more efficient irrigation techniques resulted in the salvage of water that would otherwise have been lost, without any impact on return-flow users within the basin.

In 1992 MWD also reached an agreement with irrigators of the Palo Verde Irrigation District (PVID) near the southeastern edge of the state. In this agreement, irrigators agreed to fallow their land on a rotational basis for periods of up to two years. These farmers then received approximately $1,575 for each hectare placed in fallow per year. As a result of this program, the MWD paid $20 million to receive approximately 110 million cubic meters of water per year. This program minimized, but did not eliminate, the adverse economic impact on third parties within the area.

As a follow-on to this concept, the San Diego Water Authority and the MWD agreed to cooperate with the U.S. Bureau of Reclamation in lining the All-American Canal located along the U.S.–Mexican border. This canal loses a significant amount of water into the underlying groundwater basin. The process of lining the canal has begun but has caused international tensions. Groundwater users in Mexico, immediately south of the border, have historically relied on the canal's leakage to recharge the groundwater systems on which they depend. Once again, the historic return-flow users are being threatened, and, in this instance, the international concerns will have to be addressed.

Groundwater Management

California has been at the forefront of the development of innovative laws and concepts for managing groundwater. The use of the major Southern California groundwater basins, including the San Gabriel basin, Los Angeles coastal basin, and the Raymond basin, began early, as these areas were being settled. Initially, groundwater was the major source of water for both potable and irrigation use within Southern California. Flow in the rivers was lost to the ocean because surface water flowed only during infrequent periods of flooding during the winter and rivers were totally dry during the summer. As a consequence, natural groundwater recharge during winter flows allowed development of the vast citrus industry and the settlement of Southern California.

Competition between owners of wells finally came to a head in the Raymond groundwater basin located near the City of Pasadena. As a result of major litigation, the court took jurisdiction over management of the groundwater basin and provided a system of water rights and pumping limitations within the basin. The court appointed a water master to administer the basin, and this court officer enforces and administers the water rights. This has resulted in stability, flexibility, and a form of markets for groundwater rights or pumping rights within the basin. The rental and sale of pumping rights developed, as did ground-water recharge facilities, which provide a market in recharge credits within the basin to add flexibility when pumping allocations are exceeded. This interesting groundwater management has been gradually adapted to other, much larger, basins, such as the Upper San Gabriel, San Gabriel, and Los Angeles coastal basins.

Lessons Learned

Although not all of the California examples represent premier examples of free market water transfers, they do illustrate the hazards of taking precipitous actions and indicate the potential that exists for bartering or paying for more-efficient agricultural systems in exchange for receiving a portion of the water saved. In such instances, both the original agricultural user and the purchaser receive benefits as the efficiency of the system improves. In situations where there are no return-flow beneficiaries, as in the case of the Salton Sea where the water is lost to a saline sink, the program provides benefits to all involved. However, in other instances, such as the All-American Canal, the benefits of efficiency may well be offset by losses to third-party beneficiaries. The provision of compensation or mitigation to these third-party beneficiaries must be considered as a transaction cost of the market transfer.

Within California, the concept of water markets, water banks, and bartered improvements in efficiency continues to be hotly debated. Some of the questions still facing the legislature and regulators in California are the same as those facing politicians and regulators in developing countries. Such questions include whether a water market should be free or regulated, who should benefit from the sale and transfer of water supplies that historically have been viewed as the property of the sovereign, where should environmental and ecological uses and needs for water within river systems stand in comparison with other priority uses of water, whether the market should be allowed to determine the distribution of water within the economy, and whether less-advantaged water users will be able to compete in a market environment. These questions are being considered and addressed in California, just as they will have to be addressed in the developing world.

Observations

The concept of the market process as a method of adjusting supplies to changing demands should probably be introduced when formulating a process for managing water resources, before strong vested interests have developed. In this manner, Colorado, where water markets have been considered part of the water management process for more than 150 years, has seen the evolution of relatively free unregulated markets in water and has developed a fair, while cumbersome, process of providing consideration to third-party beneficiaries. California, which had historically strongly restricted the transfer of water within a market system, is attempting to establish such a market in the face of regulators, large users, and philosophical advocates who are attempting to manipulate the development of such a market.

In 1996 an additional attempt was made to craft water transfer legislation in California. Theoretically, this "transfer act for California" would allow a more free market system to develop. The law would:

- Increase the legal protection of water transfers throughout the transfer process
- Clarify the Department of Water Resources transfer process and limit the time allowed for reviewing transfers, thus expediting the process for reviewing transfers of conserved and salvaged water
- Clarify that water dedicated to instream uses be in addition to legal requirements
- Allow local water district customers to transfer the water that they are entitled to but require that transfers be approved by the local agency
- Establish a fund to compensate injury caused by expedited transfers of conserved water
- Establish local water banks.

This proposed legislation would still result in a very controlled market with prices established by the legislative or administrative process and would require transfers to be made only to administratively sanctioned water banks. It would also require transfers to be approved by local or state agencies. Although a step in the direction of a free market, it is still a considerable distance from the relatively free market processes in Colorado and a long distance from the totally free market processes advocated by economic theorists.

These case studies provide examples of both good and bad practices and impacts of existing water markets in a well-developed scenario. However, the basic principles and concepts are equally applicable in other settings, if they are adjusted to accommodate different social, cultural, and economic conditions. Chapter 5 discusses water market experiences in other less-developed or developing scenarios.

5

Water Markets in International Perspective

Water resources management in Latin America has received relatively little attention, given that most of the countries in the region have been relatively well endowed with water in relation to their needs. This situation is rapidly changing as rapid growth of agricultural, industrial, and municipal consumption has made water a scarce resource around major cities and traditionally arid regions such as the Northeast in Brazil, much of Mexico, and along much of the Pacific Coast in Chile, Ecuador, and Peru. The rising investment and environmental costs of water resources schemes have led to a rethinking and an acceptance of the need to ensure the optimum use of available water resources. The countries in Latin America and the Caribbean are at different stages of development of their water markets and models for water resources management, which enables them to learn from those countries whose implementation of water markets and integrated water resources management is more advanced.

This chapter discusses four countries or regions. The first consists of the arid islands in the Canarias, which have a long tradition of freely functioning water markets. The second is Chile, which has made great strides in the past two decades to improve the efficiency of its water use, including the introduction of free trading in water rights. The third is Brazil, where the pace of reform in the water sector has accelerated in recent years. The same is true for Mexico, the fourth country discussed.

The Canary Islands

Tenerife and Gran Canaria located in the Canary Islands represent water markets of great relevance to Latin America and elsewhere (this section draws heavily on Mesa Hernández 1985a and 1985b and Hoyos-Limón Gil 1985). They share the same legal heritage as much of Latin America. The islands were colonized by Spain and became royal property. Over time, the Spanish kings, through their representatives, transferred ownership of some of the land and surface waters to favored individuals. Most of the land, and some of the surface water, remained royal property and later became property of the state. Groundwater belonged to anyone willing to invest in the structures needed to bring it to the surface.

The Canary Islands are similar to many regions in the Americas in the severity of their hydrology. While some of the islands receive heavy precipitation, most are arid and receive little or no precipitation. Originally surface flows were augmented by groundwater, but with drawdown of the groundwater tables, few sources presently carry surface water throughout the year. The small quantity of stormwater that does fall on the islands is mostly lost to the sea. The precarious water balance is compounded by difficult geology, because the volcanic origin of the islands has created relatively undefined aquifers where artificial groundwater recharge is not a reliable option.

Investments in Water Resources Development

Unique activities have been used to develop the scarce water resources in the Canary Islands. Although some dams and reservoirs were constructed with public funding, most of the water resources were developed exclusively with private funding. In essence, the task of finding and exploiting the available groundwater stimulated widespread investment of personal savings to construct horizontal galleries into the mountains. Development using well shafts connected by horizontal boreholes predominates on Gran Canaria, while on Tenerife this practice is augmented by many standard vertical wells. The development started in the mid-1800s and accelerated in the early part of the twentieth century to supply water for the cultivation of export cash crops. While the main cash crop is bananas, introduced in the early 1900s, cash crops now include other fruits and flowers as well.

The source of the invested funds varied. Remittances from overseas workers played a role, but modest savings from the resident population were also directed through water associations (*comunidades de aguas*) to the gradual perforation of horizontal wells. The pace of construction was slow given the simple technology available at the time. This actually favored private financing, since modest savings were sufficient to fund the gradual execution of galleries. Private funding predominated on Tenerife, while funding on Gran Canaria included additional sources.

The island of Tenerife alone has in excess of 1,500 horizontal wells and galleries. In addition, public funding and savings also constructed a system of storage reservoirs and canals that supplies groundwater to almost any point on the island. All in all, the length of the horizontal wells and galleries is about 1,700 kilometers and that of the canals is more than 4,000 kilometers. The number of storage reservoirs of different types and sizes is in excess of 8,000.

This hydraulic infrastructure was built almost entirely by private initiative with minimal interference from local authorities. It was not until 1924 that an administrative registration became compulsory to ensure that new perforations would not unduly affect existing wells and works under way.

The Utilization of Water Resources

Private entrepreneurs who risked their own and others' savings to find groundwater acquired a property right to the developed water. In effect, the water flowing out of the successful wells and galleries immediately became valuable given the ready demand of agriculturalists and other consumers. At the same time, the availability of vast conveyance works on the island of Tenerife created the conditions for a competitive market where users could compare offers from different suppliers delivering water along different routes and pay a conveyance fee to outside owners of the conveyance works. For example, on the Gran Canaria, water as well as shares or stocks in water rights are sold through three privately run water stock markets.

The *comunidades de aguas* have another unique feature: they do not hold property or exploit the water produced on behalf of their shareholders; rather, each shareholder is free to use the portion of the water to which he is entitled in any way he wishes. The owner of the water can, for instance, enter into a contract to supply a quantity of water annually or to supply water during a brief period of the year. The smooth functioning of this water market is helped by special brokers who match suppliers with clients.

As a consequence of this market system, the owner of the water produced has an incentive to use the water efficiently because its marginal cost equates to the sales price that can be obtained for it. This contrasts with the situation in countries where administrative permits are granted to extract groundwater, often without metering or rigorous monitoring. In this latter situation, the marginal cost of water extracted becomes zero, which encourages waste and overextraction.

In Tenerife, the total supply of water has grown tenfold from some 700 liters per second in the middle of the nineteenth century to close to 7,000 liters per second in 1991. The increase reflects the substantial mining of groundwater, with the result that the water produced from individual wells and galleries is slowly decreasing, and additional work is required to sink horizontal wells deeper into the ground.

The water market is highly competitive and therefore relatively efficient. On Tenerife, the *comunidades de aguas* do not sell the water themselves but distribute the production among the owners who are then free to sell their share. Thousands of sellers and buyers can supply and obtain water over different routes, given the extensive conveyance works. Water can be purchased in a number of ways. One way is simply to buy shares in a *comunidad de aguas* and obtain the pro rata share of future production. The water in shares in the *comunidad de aguas* is entirely liquid, because there are so many shareholders. Another way is to buy a given quantity over a fixed time period. Either way, the market is highly mobile and shifting. The fact that certain water sources slowly diminish in production forces buyers to be on the lookout for alternative routes.

The need for regulation has scarcely arisen because the high degree of competition safeguards against abuses. The 1990 Water Law for the Canary Islands includes a provision concerning maximum water prices that has never been applied.

Price Evolution of Bulk Water

As could be expected, the prices of bulk water have risen slowly to reflect the increasing scarcity of groundwater and the cost of going deeper underground. Table 5.1 shows the evolution of water prices corrected for inflation during the 1985–95 period. The average annual increment over this period was 0.4 percent. The slight annual increases or decreases in water prices reflect the inevitable fluctuations in rainfall and demand. The Tenerife water market did not suffer any supply difficulties of the type that the southern regions of peninsular Spain experienced in the wake of a series of dry years in the 1990s. This is principally because the peninsular regions are forced to rely on surface supplies that were greatly affected by the drought, while the islands use groundwater supplies that remained reliable and were used efficiently due to the market incentives.

Chile

The emergence of functioning water markets in Chile should be seen against the backdrop of three decades of profound and contrasting policy reforms before the present water code was adopted in 1981 (this section draws on Ríos Brehm and Quiroz 1995). The first water code,

Table 5.1   Average Bulk Water Price in Santa Cruz de Tenerife, 1985–95
(pesetas per cubic meter)

Year	Current price	Constant price	Percent increment
1985	33.0	59.4	—
1986	36.2	58.6	-1.3
1987	38.7	59.4	+1.4
1988	40.8	59.7	+0.5
1989	43.4	59.6	-0.2
1990	46.7	60.1	+0.7
1991	50.1	60.8	+1.2
1992	52.7	60.4	-0.8
1993	55.9	61.2	+1.4
1994	59.5	62.2	+1.6
1995	61.6	61.6	-1.1

— Not available.

implemented in 1951, allowed water to be transferred as long as the use remained unchanged. A distinction was made between public and private ownership of water. The state could grant concessions to private parties, and these concessions allowed the concessionaire to use the water concession much like private property. Where demand for water exceeded supply, the water was allocated by administrative fiat on the basis of a list of priorities.

The ascent of a socialist government had a profound effect on Chile's water legislation. In 1969 all surface water and groundwater were declared state property. Although the state continued to grant concessions to private parties, it could, at any time, terminate a concession without compensating the private concessionaire. The concessions could be neither transferred nor sold to another private party.

Shortly after the overturn of the socialist government in 1973, deep reforms were undertaken to make the water sector more efficient and to stimulate investments that would depend on the use of water for their economic return. The work culminated in the promulgation of the Water Code of 1981.

The Water Code of 1981

Both surface and groundwater resources are national goods for public use. However, private parties can acquire water rights that are separate from land rights, and these rights can be sold and bought like any other property under the laws of the civil code. There are two kinds of water rights: permanent rights and eventual rights. Permanent rights allow a specified volume of water to be used without restrictions, unless the flow is insufficient for all parties, in which case the available water is allocated proportionately. Eventual rights give holders the right to use only the excess water that remains after all permanent rights have been satisfied.

Both permanent and eventual rights are granted by the state with no charge except when there are competing demands for the same water, in which case the water is allocated to the highest bidder. There are no priorities in the allocation of water, and the state has a limited role in resolving conflicts. Conflicts are resolved through private negotiations and the judiciary system under the civil code.

Water rights distinguish between consumptive and nonconsumptive uses of water. Consumptive water rights enable the holder to use all the water without obligation to return any portion. A typical example would be agricultural, industrial, and domestic demand. Nonconsumptive water rights oblige the holder to return the same amount of a stipulated quality of water back to the stream. A good example would be the water used to generate hydroelectric energy. Between one-third and half of all water rights are traditional rights that have not been legalized or acquired property title. These rights are based on long usage that has been thoroughly respected.

The General Directorate of Water (Dirección General de Aguas) in the Ministry of Public Works is responsible for planning water resources and for granting water rights. Much of the detailed work involved in distributing and enforcing the correct use of water falls to water user associations. These associations also collect fees for the construction, maintenance, and administration of all irrigation infrastructure. About 300,000 water users are grouped in some 4,000 water user associations.

Nonconsumptive uses account for about 68 percent of all water used, followed by the consumptive uses of agriculture (28 percent), municipal water supplies (2 percent), and industry and mining (2 percent).

Activities of Water Markets

The 1981 Water Code allows complete freedom to trade water rights of different kinds. One study reports on about 600 water transactions that took place over a one-year period, 1993–94, in the Santiago area (Rosegrant and Gazmuri 1994). The large majority (94 percent) of the negotiations were between farmers, whereas about 3 percent were between farmers and urban water supply and sewerage companies, and

1 percent were between farmers and mining companies. As could be expected, water markets were more active in regions where water was relatively more scarce. For instance, the proportion of total water flow traded was about 3 percent in the drier central Santiago region, but less than 1 percent in the more southern Bulnes region, with higher rainfall.

Efficiency gains have undoubtedly resulted from the growth of water trading. The market in permanent rights has, for instance, allowed farmers to sell part of their water shares to towns and cities that, in turn, have saved themselves from having to capture and bring more water into their service area. Similarly, the large spot market in which irrigation water is rented for periods of different duration has similarly provided a flexible instrument that enables farmers to use water in the most optimal fashion.

Water trading has brought environmental gains as well. Farmers typically sell only a portion of their water shares to water supply utilities and use the proceeds to invest in water-saving irrigation equipment. As a result, they are able to maintain or increase their crop production using less water but more capital investment. The greater efficiency places less strain on the environment, because additional investments in water supply can be deferred.

Observed Problems

As might be expected, the implementation of water markets has not been without friction. The most serious conflict has been between consumptive and nonconsumptive uses of water. At first, it was thought that the two uses would not conflict with one another because nonconsumptive users were obliged to replenish the water after using it. In practice, a clear conflict exists and has worked to the detriment of consumptive users downstream of the upstream nonconsumptive users. The major nonconsumptive use of water is to generate hydroelectric energy. Invariably, the water reservoirs are not filled in such a fashion as to ensure that downstream uses are unaffected. For example, consumptive users located downstream could lay claim to water trapped by reservoirs during the dry season, so the timing of use has created conflicts. Moreover, the water used for power generation rarely is restored to the point immediately downstream of the reservoir. Water is frequently released well downstream of the diversion point, and, as a consequence, intermediate users suffer. Efforts to safeguard the flora and fauna downstream of the reservoir may also suffer. The fact that a given river carries less water during the dry season also implies that less water is available to dilute pollution downstream of the reservoir.

Another conflict has arisen because a large share of the nonconsumptive rights were given to hydroelectric companies following the 1981 Water Code. These, often unused, water rights are felt to block new development involving other uses, both nonconsumptive and consumptive. This has been viewed as speculation in water rights because the unused water rights were captured and registered free of charge and without any commitment to use the water in the foreseeable future and without a beneficial-use test.

Proposals have been made to amend the 1981 Water Code so that the holders of water rights are obliged to use them within five years or else forfeit them. There are also legislative proposals to consider environmental and other external costs related to the water released from hydroelectric and other dams. These proposals include taxing unused rights in an attempt to force holders to relinquish them. These remedial measures probably could have been avoided if the original allocation had considered the potential for development or beneficial use. However, given the political and economic strength of the energy and mining firms now holding these rights, the situation will be difficult to change.

From a broader point of view, implementation of the water market in Chile has been successful and, as has been the case in North America, the law will undoubtedly continue to evolve to accommodate the changing demands of Chilean society.

Brazil

From a general standpoint, the legal and regulatory framework for water resource management is evolving in Brazil. The ownership of all water rests with the sovereign, as it does in most other countries in the Americas. The federal constitution gives the federal government jurisdiction over water in interstate or international rivers but assigns control of water in intrastate rivers to the respective states. The recent passage of a new federal water law reinforces this concept and provides the foundation for each state to formulate water laws relevant to its waters. The federal law also clarifies the responsibilities for a federal water resource strategy in the Secretariat of Water Resources within the Ministry of Environment, Water Resources, and the Legal Amazon. This eliminates a great deal of duplication within the federal government and clearly empowers the states to formulate policy for waters within their jurisdiction.

A number of states have adopted or are in the process of formulating new water laws, several of which include a framework for a water market. The primary objective for the states at present is to implement strong water rights and allocation systems, strong administrative systems to enforce, measure, register, and administer water rights, and strong public information efforts to make the general public and users aware of the value of water and the right to its use. This effort should result in a broad general knowledge of water conservation and efficient water use and, eventually, convince the public of the beneficial role of the market process. Throughout Brazil, there is broad acceptance of the importance of the nation's water resources. This should, in turn, result in greater emphasis on the development and use of water in a manner that benefits the Brazilian economy and society.

State of Ceará

Specifically, the State of Ceará in the Northeast Region of Brazil has made great strides toward adopting a system for allocating, registering, and enforcing water rights. A water resource management project, partially financed by the World Bank, assisted in the adoption of a comprehensive water law that instituted a system of water rights. This formal system replaced a completely informal system where the right to use water was prescribed by the strongest user. The federal government through the Departamento Nacional de Obras Contra as Secas had constructed numerous dams and reservoirs within the state. These reservoirs were used to store water during the rainy season, and that water was released to the normally dry streambeds during dry periods to "perennialize" the rivers. The water released in such a manner was available to any and all users as often as it appeared in the rivers. No limit was placed on the amount of water that could be diverted from these flows, and users high on the rivers could divert the entire flow if they had sufficient land or capacity to do so. In fact, on occasions the entire flow of the perennialized river was diverted immediately below the federal structure from which it had been released, to the detriment of all other users on the river.

Under the new law, water rights are being issued within the state based on historic beneficial use, are being registered, and will be enforced. Bulk water use charges are being instituted for all users, and these charges will support the administration of the water rights system as well as the sustainable operation and maintenance of the basinwide infrastructure used to store and manage the bulk water of river systems.

The water resource management project also includes a component to study and, eventually, pilot a market-based water rights transfer system to enable the system to adjust more flexibly to changing demands and to shift water to the highest-value uses during times of shortages. While water for human consumption is given preference over all other uses, a market-based system could provide a means for exercising that preference so that all users are compensated and preference is truly used only for human consumption. In the past, when a large municipality ran short of water during a drought, through the lack of either sufficient supplies or proper conservation, the needed water was expropriated by fiat from agriculture without compensation. The studies to be conducted as a part of this project will attempt to devise a politically and socially acceptable mechanism using market processes to redistribute water during droughts. This will be combined with an integrated management project that will optimize scarce water supplies between river basins within the state. The ongoing water resource management project and the integrated basin management project are part of a long-range water resources strategy that, when combined with a market-based reallocation mechanism, should optimize the use of native water within the state over the next 15 years.

Cariri

An area in the State of Ceará—Cariri—receives its water from spring-fed streams that derive water from natural recharge on the adjacent Chapada do Araripe, a high plateau (this discussion draws on Kemper, Yarley de Brito Gonçalves, and Brito Bezerra 1996). This plateau is covered with desert brush and tree vegetation with some subsistence farming. The recharge typically occurs during the summer rainy seasons of January through June as runoff percolates into the underlying permeable sandstone and moves laterally along an impermeable formation until it exits in the form of springs along the escarpment below the plateau. Approximately 300 springs emanate from the plateau, with 250 on the Ceará side of the escarpment. Flows from the springs are influenced largely by the variability of rainfall on the plateau, with some attenuation from year to year as a result of natural storage. These springs produce an average of approximately 40 million cubic meters of water per year. This region is primarily agricultural and has typically produced sugarcane. Although once completely rural, it is now the location of developing municipalities such as Juazeiro do Norte, Barbalho, Jardim, and Crato. These municipalities have historically used the highest-yielding springs and artesian wells as their source of water.

An interesting water rights system has developed in the Batateira spring. Water use from this spring was formalized by a contract among the users in 1854. The water rights from the spring were originally bought from the municipality of Crato under this contract, and the documentation of this transfer was formalized in the official records of the city. Although this transfer and its records could be questioned under past and present law, the rights of use have been respected historically as prescriptive rights. The transferred rights were divided between the original 14 landholders along the river based on the amount of land under irrigation; they were originally distributed through peer cooperation. The return flows from the allocations could be used by downstream users, but these return flows were not guaranteed. This has minimized the inflexibility of third-party impacts on market transfers of water use rights in the area.

The rights within the stream were originally divided into increments called *telhas,* defined as the amount of water that could flow through a standard-size (18-centimeter-diameter) clay pipe with a slope of 1:1,000. In more common terms, a *telha* amounts to a flow of approximately 64 cubic meters per hour. The spring was measured so that the equivalent yield in *telhas* could be determined, and that amount was then allocated. The original rights of the Batateira spring were held as 23 full *telhas.* The original allocation reserved 1 *telha* of flow to preserve a minimum streamflow in the river emanating from the spring. However, as average flows decreased over time, this concept was abandoned. During times of shortage and now that flows in the spring have declined, a priority system gives higher priority to the rights located highest on the river. Each right on the river diverts and uses its entitlement until no more water is available. The lower rights then receive no water. This unusual system of priorities was stipulated in the original contract of 1854 and was recently upheld by the local court when controversies arose regarding the rights of downstream users.

Over the years, there has also been a policy that the water is not tied to the land and is fungible. There have been numerous transactions between the holders of the rights and users with higher-value demands. Over the years, the rights have become divided as succeeding generations have split their family holdings. The rights are now subdivided by time and flow and are measured in *telha*-hours. For example, transactions now take place for the right to a certain number of *telha*-hours per week or for a certain number of *telha*-hours twice or three times a week.

To complicate the system even further, certain older rights receive the right to the full flow of the spring during weekend periods, while the rest of the system operates only during weekdays. It is impossible to determine whether these special rights were purchased from other farmers through the market process, but they are honored by the other farmers. One example of a water transfer is the acquisition in 1925 of 12 hours of 3 *telhas* each day during weekdays to support a water mill. This right changed hands for 2,000 blocks of *rapadura,* or raw brown sugar. In a more recent transaction in 1993, the right to 58 hours of 3 *telhas* every second weekend was purchased for the equivalent of $40,000 in cattle and *cachaça,* a distilled sugarcane liquor.

Over the past 50 years, the average yield of the Batateira spring has gradually decreased. This can probably be attributed to land use practices in the recharge area of the plateau such as overgrazing, woodcutting, and slash-and-burn farming. This type of use has probably increased runoff and erosion during rainy periods and decreased the capacity of the soil to accept the percolation of recharge water. As a consequence, the average yield of the Batateira spring for agricultural use has diminished from 23 *telhas* (1,479 cubic meters per hour) to about 5.8 *telhas* (373 cubic meters per hour).

The administration and management of the system are strictly at the user level, with each user monitoring the use of others within each spring system, making sure that each user is taking only the water within his right. Each user has a *levadeiro,* or employee, who is responsible for assuring that the rights of the user are monitored and that he is receiving his full entitlement. In some, infrequent, instances the *levadeiros* have been bribed to look the other way as interlopers used the water or rightful users took water out of turn. In such instances, policing has been carried out by the users themselves. The system is also maintained on a cooperative and joint basis, with each use sharing in proportion to the entitlement.

This user-based system was developed on a cooperative and peer-administered basis and continues to operate with little corruption or controversy. Although the market system is obviously quite limited, users have opted for a market-oriented system without the stimulus of outside interests or pressures. It will be interesting to observe how this market functions as the region's growing municipalities expand their demand for water. Because the state law in Ceará places the use of water for human needs ahead of all other uses, it will be interesting to see if the market is used to satisfy the expanding municipal needs as opposed to legislative or administrative fiat.

Bahia and Rio Grande do Norte

Embryonic water management and water market strategies are also being used in the states of Bahia and Rio Grande do Norte, where new water laws define a process for issuing, registering, and administering water use rights. The laws in these states also provide for the eventual establishment of market-based transfer mechanisms for reallocating water use rights to meet changing demands and droughts. World Bank–financed water resource management projects are being developed to assist in this effort in many other states, and World Bank–financed technical assistance has been instrumental in the progress and preparation achieved to date. It is anticipated that a strong market-based transfer process will result from these projects as demands continue to evolve and pressures to change uses to meet new needs continue to develop.

Mexico

In 1992 Mexico adopted a new water law that established market-based transfers of water use concessions, subject to approval by the administrative authorities of government. Although the Comisión Nacional de Agua (CNA) has accepted the market transfer concept in principle, it still retains strong authority over intersectoral transfers, interbasin transfers, and any transfers that might create adverse environmental impacts. It can be anticipated that water market transfers in these areas will be closely scrutinized and will be subject to considerable regulation and conditions. Market processes in these areas will evolve slowly and will occur only after strong demand has been expressed and the market has been reviewed carefully at both the administrative and judicial level.

Mexico uses the proportional appropriation doctrine, in which each right is entitled to a proportionate amount of the water available within the respective basin or river system each year. These rights are generally issued on the basis of full consumption, with the rights to return flows reserved for the holder of the right. This has minimized the prescription of rights to return flows and the potential for third-party impacts as a result of the removal of return flows. However, where historical use of return flows has existed for years prior to implementation of the new law and new allocation system, third-party damages will probably be strongly contested in the event of market transfers. This law also decentralizes the system, giving user organizations the responsibility for operating and maintaining irrigation systems. Historically, the control of water use rights and concessions was centralized at the federal level. Although the new law advocates decentralization, the cultural tradition of centralized control has not been eliminated, and control has generally moved to the regional CNA level. The responsibility for operation and maintenance has, however, generally been transferred. With the continued change in political climate and the increasing strength of user associations, the status quo is changing gradually.

To date, market transactions for water use rights, both permanent and on an annual rental basis, have predominately occurred within user associations and irrigation systems. The control of this type of transaction rests with user associations, and this has facilitated acceptance at the peer level. The development of permanent water use transfers has been inhibited to some degree because the national register is not complete, so title to the rights may not inspire confidence in the marketplace. In addition, many of the water use rights are issued to the irrigation district or to a portion of the irrigation district, rather than to individual farmers. Consequently, individual rights can be transferred only within the irrigation district. Any transfer of use rights outside the district would require the acquiescence of all users or, at least, the management of the district. In addition, the approval of the regional office of the CNA would be required for transfers between sectors or basins. These issues are being examined as regulations under the new water law are being revised.

The potential of the market-based process within Mexico is evident in the transfer of water from farmers using water from the Chichimequilas Aquifer to the City Water Company of Querétaro. In this example, the city paid for 70 percent of the improvements to the irrigation system (the users organization paid the balance) in exchange for a portion of the water saved through the improvements. This intersectoral transfer of water resembles the arrangements being used in Southern California by the MWD and the IID. It is anticipated that, as water use rights become accepted as economic assets, the concept of market-based transfers of these rights will also gain acceptance. Also, as the pressures of changing demands increase, there is a strong possibility that market mechanisms, rather than political and administrative fiat, will be used to effect transfers. It is also anticipated that empowerment of the user associations will gradually offset centralized administrative control at the national and regional level and further advance the use of market mechanisms. However, the same types of controversies and opposition from indirect impacts and peripheral beneficiaries will probably develop in this system. Dispute resolution mechanisms will have to be refined, and impact mitigation measures will have to be considered as these market processes develop.

Bibliography

The word "processed" describes informally reproduced works that may not be commonly available through library systems.

Hearne, Robert R., and K. William Easter. 1995. *Water Allocation and Water Markets: An Analysis of Gains-from-Trade in Chile.* World Bank Technical Paper 315. Washington, D.C.: World Bank.

Hill, David G. 1993. "Water Law Confusion." Boulder, Colo. Processed.

Hobbs, Gregory J. 1997. "Historical Perspective on Western Land and Water Law." Paper presented at the Colorado River Compact Symposium, Santa Fe, New Mexico. Processed.

Hoyos-Limón Gil, Adolfo. 1985. "La utilización de aguas subterráneas en Canarias y su papel económico, social y de oportunidad." Processed.

Kemper, Karin, José Yarley de Brito Gonçalves, and Francisco Willian Brito Bezerra. 1996. "Water Allocation and Trading in the Cariri Region: Ceará, Brazil." World Bank, Fortaleza. Processed.

McCarthy, Elizabeth. 1995. *Water Marketing and Transfers.* Sacramento: Water Education Foundation.

———. 1995. *Water Rights Law.* Sacramento: Water Education Foundation.

Mesa Hernández, C. Jesus. 1985a. "Communicación de XIII Congreso Europeo de Derecho Agrario." Paper presented at the XIII European Congress of Agrarian Rights, Santa Cruz de Tenerife. Processed.

———. 1985b. "Economía y mercados de aguas subterráneas en Canarias en relación con la planificación hídrica." Processed.

Ríos Brehm, Monica, and Jorge Quiroz Castro. 1995. *The Market of Water Rights in Chile: Outstanding Issues.* World Bank Technical Paper 285. Washington, D.C.: World Bank.

Rosegrant, Mark W., and Renato S. Gazmuri. 1994. "Reforming Water Allocation Policy through Markets in Tradable Water Rights: Lessons from Chile, Mexico, and California." EPTD Discussion Paper 6. Environment and Production Technology Division, International Food Policy Research Institute, Washington, D.C. Processed.

Tyler, Daniel. 1992. *The Last Water Hole in the West.* Niwot: University Press of Colorado.

Vranesh, George. 1985. *Colorado Water Law.* Boulder, Colo.: George Vranish Publications.

World Bank. 1993. *Water Resources Management.* World Bank Policy Paper. Washington, D.C.